W9-BVM-934

THE DECLINE OF ANCIENT INDIAN CIVILIZATION

KERRY HINTON

ROSEN
PUBLISHING®
New York

Published in 2017 by The Rosen Publishing Group, Inc.
29 East 21st Street, New York, NY 10010

Copyright © 2017 by The Rosen Publishing Group, Inc.

First Edition

Library of Congress Cataloging-in-Publication Data

Names: Hinton, Kerry, author.
Title: The decline of ancient Indian civilization / Kerry Hinton.
Description: First edition. | New York : Rosen Publishing, 2017. | Series: Spotlight on the rise and fall of ancient civilizations | Includes bibliographical references and index. | Audience: Grades 7-12.
Identifiers: LCCN 2016000812| ISBN 9781477789285 (library bound) | ISBN 9781477789261 (pbk.) | ISBN 9781477789278 (6-pack)
Subjects: LCSH: India--Civilization--To 1200. | India--History--To 324 B.C. | India--History--324 B.C.-1000 A.D.
Classification: LCC DS425 .H56 2016 | DDC 934/.01--dc23
LC record available at http://lccn.loc.gov/2016000812

Manufactured in the United States of America

CONTENTS

WHERE IS INDIA?   4

INDIA'S PAST   6

THE INDUS RIVER VALLEY CIVILIZATION   8

THE VEDIC PERIOD I   12

THE VEDIC PERIOD II   14

THE PERSIANS ARRIVE   18

THE GREEK INVASION   20

THE MAURYAN EMPIRE   22

THE DARK AGE   26

THE RISE OF THE GUPTA EMPIRE   28

THE GOLDEN AGE OF INDIA   32

THE DECLINE AND FALL OF THE GUPTA EMPIRE   34

FROM MUSLIM RULE TO THE 20TH CENTURY   38

INDIA TODAY   40

GLOSSARY   42

FOR MORE INFORMATION   43

FOR FURTHER READING   45

BIBLIOGRAPHY   46

INDEX   47

WHERE IS INDIA?

The Indian subcontinent is in southern Asia. This large piece of land extends from the Himalayas to the Indian Ocean. Today, it includes India, Pakistan, and Nepal.

The country of India is a peninsula, extending to the southernmost tip of the subcontinent and into the Indian Ocean. To either side are the Arabian Sea and the Bay of Bengal.

Almost all types of terrain exist here. The mountains, deserts and rainforests of this landmass are also in between two of the largest rivers in the world: the Indus and the Ganges. This location has made India an important center of trade for the last five thousand years.

At its height, ancient India stretched across 2 million square miles (5,179, 976 square kilometers) and had more inhabitants than modern Australia and North Korea combined. Much has changed since then, but India and its people have been very important to the culture and development of our world.

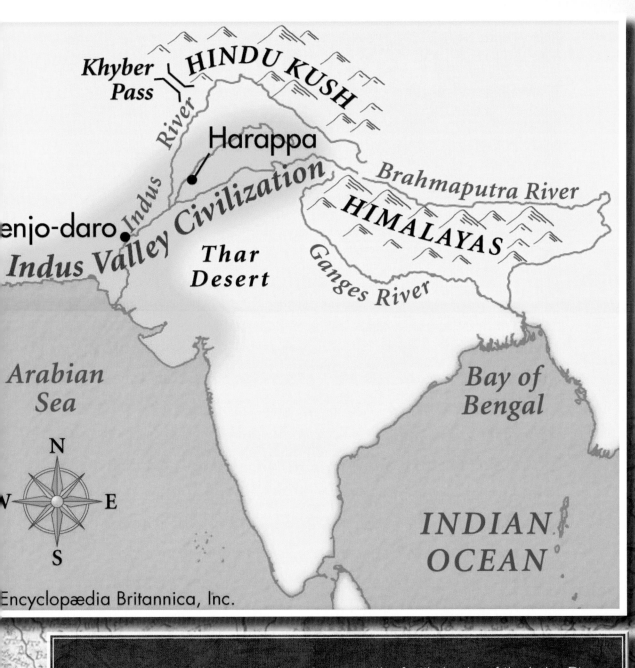

Khyber
Pass

HINDU KUSH

Indus River

Harappa

Brahmaputra River

HIMALAYAS

enjo-daro

Indus Valley Civilization

Thar
Desert

Ganges River

Arabian
Sea

N

W   E

S

Bay of
Bengal

INDIAN
OCEAN

Encyclopædia Britannica, Inc.

The Indus Valley civilization made its home on the fertile banks of the Indus River on the modern-day border between India and Pakistan.

INDIA'S PAST

Fossils show that human beings lived on the Indian subcontinent as long as seventy-five thousand years ago.

Along with Egypt, China, and Mesopotamia, India was one of the great civilizations of the ancient world.

Early settlers of India came from Africa. They were nomads who moved from place to place in small groups. They travelled through Arabia to reach the Indian subcontinent. Many passed through over the years.

Around 5000 BCE, some nomads decided to stay and live in one place — the Indus River Valley. The Indus River is one of the longest rivers in the world. The land nearby was very fertile, which made it possible to settle down, grow crops, and raise livestock. Today, it covers parts of western India and eastern Pakistan.

As the settlers began to move away from a mobile existence, they began to also build structures and societies that were not as temporary.

Ancient nomads traveled over the land from place to place, eventually remaining in the hospitable region of the Indus River Valley.

THE INDUS RIVER VALLEY CIVILIZATION

On the banks of the Indus River, the small villages started by nomads became towns and cities. These cities began to trade ideas and goods with one another.

At the height of this civilization, over 1,500 cities dotted the Indus Valley. Some were larger and more advanced than cities in China and Egypt.

The Indus Civilization was very advanced. Many homes had bathrooms and wells for clean water. The people had advanced tools and learned how to store food. They also developed a language made of drawings called pictographs. Many were farmers—they grew wheat, peas, melons, and dates and raised cattle, sheep, and pigs.

By 3000 BCE, regular trade began with other early civilizations such as Mesopotamia. (Today, this region is known as the countries of Iraq, Syria, and Kuwait.)

Large communal wells made of stone provided water for drinking, bathing, and laundering in the early cities of Harappa and Mohenjo-Daro.

At first, different cultures traded rare and valuable items that they could not find at home. This exchange of spices, textiles, and metals provided an example for other civilizations to follow.

Soon, many cities were trading with one another over many continents. This is the first time in human history that people traded over such great distances.

By 1900 BCE, the Indus Civilization had begun to decline as trade with other countries slowed down. People began to leave the larger cities.

Today, this civilization's decline is still a mystery. Some scientists believe that either a flood or drought made it hard to farm and graze, forcing the inhabitants to leave. If this is true, it could explain why this once fertile river valley has a completely different climate today.

Much of the information we have about this civilization is very new. Some of the Indus Valley cities were not discovered until the 1920s. The ruins of Harappa and other cities have shown archaeologists a very accomplished society.

Farmers of the Indus Valley Civilization grew wheat, barley, and other crops that they stored in large structures called grain elevators.

THE VEDIC PERIOD I

A few centuries after the Indus Valley had been abandoned, Indo-Europeans began to migrate into India. They came from Central Asia through the Khyber Pass. These travelers brought a new animal with them—the horse. In time, horses would give them the ability to travel greater distances, farm land, and expand their society.

Indo-Europeans made other great contributions to Indian culture. Their language, Sanskrit, later developed into Hindi, which today is spoken by almost three hundred million people.

Before this, the Indo-Europeans roamed Indus Valley and fed their pigs, sheep and goats. Herding animals were very valuable—so much so that they became the currency of the society. Cattle were most valuable and were usually owned by the wealthy.

Indo-Europeans lived in small tribes ruled by warlords. These clans often fought over territory and livestock. People in these tribes had jobs, including warriors and farmers.

This stone seal from the Indus Valley civilization is carved with a picture of a cow. The animals were highly valuable and were prized in society.

THE VEDIC PERIOD II

The Indo-Europeans also brought their religion. It was based on four books called Vedas, which contain stories, songs, and prayers. Some came from older Indus River Valley religions but added new ideas and gods.

The Vedas discuss history, mythology, and religious rules to be followed in daily life. For hundreds of years, the Vedas were passed down by word of mouth. Eventually, they were written down and shared among more people.

Technology and trade increased along the Khyber Pass. The arrival of the wheel sped development as well. By 1200 BCE, the Indo-Europeans had mastered making iron, which they used for weapons and farming tools.

Vedic society expanded, creating more wealth. These new riches sprouted new cities. The clans of old disappeared and were replaced by kingdoms. The rulers of these kingdoms, however, were frequently elected by a council that represented the people.

The Rigveda is the oldest of the four Vedas of ancient India. This collection of hymns and rituals was likely written around 1200 BCE and is one of the most important Hindu texts.

These kingdoms were called *janapadas* and began to appear in about 1200 BCE. By 600 BCE, these realms had grown into even larger independent kingdoms known as *mahajanapadas*. The prefix "maja" means "great."

Sixteen mahajanapadas covered most of northern India and Pakistan. Many had collected taxes, built highways, and had individual armies.

Sometimes they would battle one another but did not take prisoners or land. Instead, the winning kingdom would often collect money from the losing one.

The caste system also began during this period. Castes were four divisions that determined a person's position in society. In most cases, a person's birth determined this, making moving to a higher caste extremely difficult.

Priests (called Brahmins) and warriors (Kshatriyas) were of a higher caste than traders or farm workers.

There was another group that were considered below all: the Untouchables (Dalits). These men and women were given the worst jobs, such as burying the dead and working with sewage.

More hymns in the Rigveda are dedicated to the ancient fire god Agni than any other deity.

THE PERSIANS ARRIVE

I n 558 BCE, the Achaemenid Empire reached the Indus River from the west. It was led by Cyrus the Great of Persia. Cyrus had already conquered most of the populated lands from the Mediterranean Sea to South Asia.

Cyrus was the first ruler to declare all men equal. He did not make slaves of the people he conquered. He rebuilt their temples and respected their customs. This new philosophy of human rights spread around the world and even inspired America's founding fathers when they were building the United States.

The modern idea of government began under Cyrus. His reign marked the first time people of different races, languages, and religions lived in different countries under one central authority. Cyrus's empire also created the world's first postal system and some of the world's first public parks.

Cyrus' ideas would prove to have a tremendous influence on India's future empires.

Cyrus the Great founded the Achaemenid Empire, which stretched from the Indus River Valley to Eastern Europe.

THE GREEK INVASION

Like Cyrus the Great, Alexander of Macedon dreamed of empire. When Alexander was twenty, his father the king was assassinated, leaving the brilliant young general the throne.

Alexander began a three year war against the Achaemenid Empire. When the battlefields cleared, he controlled all of Persia. Like Cyrus, Alexander the Great reached the Indus River in 326 BCE.

After conquering some kingdoms, Alexander continued east, but the Nanda Empire blocked his progress. The Nandas had replaced many of the Vedic mahajanapadas and now controlled most of northern India. They had great wealth and an army of thousands of men and elephants.

Alexander's men were exhausted from years of war and refused to fight. Believing they would lose, they convinced Alexander to turn south and follow the Indus River instead.

The cities he conquered or founded were still under his rule, varying the cultural influences of the region even more.

Alexander the Great defeated King Porus at the Battle of the Hydaspes in 326 BCE. Porus fought so bravely that Alexander allowed him to rule the Punjab region after the battle.

THE MAURYAN EMPIRE

The Nandas prevented Alexander's conquest but had become very unpopular. They had continued to raise taxes, making their subjects poorer. By the time Alexander left India, they were ready for new leadership.

A young warrior named Chandragupta Maurya raised an army and reclaimed the cities under Macedonian rule. He then forced the Nandas into exile and began the Mauryan Empire.

Chandragupta Maurya believed that working together, people could create a better society. He united almost all of South Asia for the first time. He encouraged religious tolerance and the arts. Instead of invading other nations, he used his army to protect his subjects. These years were some of most peaceful on the subcontinent.

The Mauryan Empire reached its peak under Chandragupta's grandson. Ashoka was a great military commander and continued to the south and west in order to bring more of South Asia under one ruler.

When Chandragupta Maurya founded the Mauryan Empire, he united most of the northern subcontinent for the first time.

After capturing the province of Kalinga, however, Ashoka's life changed completely. He saw so much bloodshed he gave up violence and converted to Buddhism.

Buddhism used some ideas from the Vedas but combined them with religious values and a philosophy of tolerance and nonviolence.

For the remainder of his life, Ashoka never started a war.

Ashoka applied his new way of life to his governing. He always sought to protect life. He ended the slave trade and banned hunting. Ashoka also showed his love of animals by starting the first animal hospitals.

Outside his kingdom, Ashoka began using the Khyber Pass for trade instead of war. He signed trade treaties with Greece and other nations. He also sent religious messengers to help Buddhism spread to other countries.

Despite his desire to share Buddhism with others, Ashoka still allowed people the freedom to practice Hinduism and other religions as they pleased.

Today, five hundred million men and women embrace Buddhism around the world.

Like his grandfather Chandragupta, King Ashoka continued to expand the Mauryan Empire until the fierce battle of Kaling. Afterward, he gave up violence and converted to Buddhism.

THE DARK AGE

After Ashoka's death, the Mauryan Empire did not survive long. In 185 BCE, Ashoka's grandson was murdered by one of his closest generals. Afterward, the empire split into many smaller kingdoms and empires. Each kingdom sought to grow larger, which created problems with boundaries. As a result, fighting began as different dynasties warred with one another.

The rulers of this time were unable to unify the subcontinent as the Mauryans had done. Without a large army, India also faced many invaders from outside. Nomadic fighters from Central and Western Asia all invaded and did their best to conquer the Indus Valley and beyond.

Although there was more conflict, India's economy continued to increase. By 300 CE, it was one of the largest in the world. The number of people practicing Hinduism on the subcontinent also grew. Gradually, these days would end and give birth to the greatest era India had known.

Maharashtra, a region in western India, has more ancient caves than any other state in the country. Many were uses for religious worships by both Buddhist and Hindu priests.

THE RISE OF THE GUPTA EMPIRE

During the Dark Age, some kingdoms were able to unify larger portions of northern India than others. One of these clans were the Kushan. They ruled in northwest India and controlled many land trade routes.

Though they were outsiders, the Kushan eventually adopted many of the manners and customs of Indian society.

The large number of opportunities for trade made many merchants rich. India was now a vital part of the Silk Road, a series of pathways that enabled goods from Europe to reach China by land, sea, or a combination of the two. The Silk Road helped spread the teachings of Buddhism as well as silk and rare spices.

The Kushans fell to Persian invaders in the third century, but the money from trade had created powerful and wealthy families who wanted to reclaim India. The Guptas were one of these families.

Large plaques made of terra-cotta were often used to cover large domes called stupas, which were used for Buddhist worship and meditation.

Through a combination of war and political agreements, the Guptas founded the greatest dynasty since the fall of the Mauryans.

The Guptas wanted their rule to reflect the great days and accomplishments of the Mauryan Empire. They chose the same capital city, Pataliputra, and their first emperor named himself Chandragupta I after the first ruler of the Mauryans.

The Guptas had many political similarities to the Mauryans. They believed a strong nation came from a strong administration.

They gave provinces the freedom to make decisions on matters that did not affect the empire as a whole. They also shared the Mauryan idea of a less violent and warlike society.

Samudrahupta, Chandragupta's son, pushed further south and added more territory to the empire. His son, Chandragupta II, ruled during the peak of the Gupta Empire and captured even more lands. As the empire expanded, the people flourished.

This was the Golden Age of India.

Some of the greatest art of ancient India was made during the Gupta Era (320-550 CE). In addition to art, great progress was made in science, astronomy, and literature.

THE GOLDEN AGE OF INDIA

The next two hundred years saw an enormous outpouring of culture, art, and science throughout the Gupta Empire. Art, literature, science, and architecture all thrived during the Golden Age. The Ramayana and Mahabharata, the greatest epic poems in India's history, were written. A playwright named Kalidasa wrote plays that are still studied today. Bronze and iron Buddhist sculpture was at the height of its popularity, also.

The Guptas were Buddhist, but they encouraged religious freedom. During their reign, Hinduism continued to grow and make new converts in India and beyond. It would eventually become the most popular religion in India.

Great strides were also made in science and astronomy. Indian mathematicians invented the numbers pi and zero. They also worked with the early decimal system. These concepts were used by architects and engineers to build wonderful temples and caves that were shrines to various Hindu gods and goddesses.

The Mahabharata is the longest epic poem written in the history of the world. It tells the story of ancient India.

THE DECLINE AND FALL OF THE GUPTA EMPIRE

Though the Guptas ruled a large, prosperous empire, they had many problems that would lead to the fall of their empire. Trade with other nation-states also slowed down. This reduced the empire's wealth and made it difficult to cover expenses. Some provinces declared their independence from the Guptas, which only weakened the central government more.

After the death of Chandragupta II in 410 CE, enemies began to invade India from all directions. Many different clans and tribes all wanted to claim India. Defending all of these invasions put the Guptas' finances under a heavy strain and added to their troubles.

During their reign, the Guptas never had control of the Khyber Pass and were unable to prevent invaders from entering India. There were many different groups trying to claim India, but the White Huns were the strongest.

Chandragupta II is depicted on this gold coin. After the great leader's death, India became vulnerable to attack from its many enemies.

The White Huns were members of a warrior clan from Central Asia. They controlled much of the land between their home and northwest India.

In about 455 CE the White Huns invaded but were defeated by Skandagupta, the Golden Age's last great leader. He drove the White Huns east and out of India. His subjects appreciated it so much they wrote songs in his honor.

After his death of their great leader in 467, the Gupta Empire continued to suffer. The rulers who came after Skandagupta couldn't keep the empire together as before. Some fought with each other, while some fought invaders. In short, the Gupta Empire was too big for them to manage.

The White Huns returned with more warriors and finally conquered the northwest. They destroyed dozens of cities as they killed and burned their way east to the Ganges.

India was fragmented once more. Some provinces remained as subjects of the Huns. By 650, the Gupta Empire had collapsed for good.

The White Huns eventually controlled much of northern India between the Indus and Ganges Rivers.

FROM MUSLIM RULE TO THE 20TH CENTURY

In 712, Muhammad bin Qasim invaded the land that is Pakistan today. The Khyber Pass led him to the wealth of India. The kingdoms of the Guptas were transformed into city-states and sultanates.

Under Muslim rule, trade continued with nations around the world. Religious tolerance kept Indian religions and customs alive and much progress was made in science and mathematics.

This lasted for almost one thousand years until the Maratha warriors from the west of India defeated the Muslims in the late 1600s and reinstated Indian rule.

The next conqueror of India would be a company, rather than invaders. In 1757, The British East India Company took control of the entire subcontinent for the next one hundred years. The British government took control until 1947, when they split the subcontinent into India and Pakistan. For the first time since the Guptas, India was independent.

After almost one hundred years of colonial rule, the British Empire gave control of the Indian subcontinent back to its people in 1947. The land was split into modern India and Pakistan.

INDIA TODAY

India's access to trade routes has made it a target of invasions for thousands of years. Because of this, many different cultures brought their ideas to India from around the world. In return, India shared its own art and religion with the world outside the subcontinent.

Modern India is the result of thousands of years of cultural contributions from dozens of different groups, including nomads, White Huns, and Muslims to name a few. Their contributions all helped create an ancient world that accomplished incredible feats of engineering, culture, science, and warfare.

Today, India shares the subcontinent with six nations. India is the second most populated country in the world, and its one billion citizens vote and speak more than fifty languages.

The lessons learned from ancient Indian kingdoms and societies have all contributed to an understanding of the ideas that make humanity as great as it can be.

Modern India maintains a connection to its ancient history through the Great Stupa of Sanchi, a domelike structure that dates back to the 3rd Century BCE.

GLOSSARY

archaeologist A person who studies fossils and other things left behind by people long ago.

Buddhism A religion started in ancient India that preaches nonviolence and kindness.

caste A system that decides placement by birth.

civilization The society and culture of a large group of people in a geographic area.

conquest To take control of a city or country by force.

date A sweet fruit that comes from palm trees.

dynasty A group of people, usually a family, that rules an empire or kingdom for many years.

empire A group of countries or a large area of land controlled by one person or group.

fertile Able to grow a large variety of crops.

geography The study of the earth's deserts, mountains, and other physical features.

graze To feed on grass or plants.

livestock Farm animals such as cows, pigs, goats, and sheep.

mainland A large piece of land that makes up a continent.

migrate To move to another country or continent.

nomad A person who has no permanent home and travels from place to place, usually for grazing land for cows and sheep.

peninsula Land surrounded by water except for a piece of land that connects it to the mainland.

pictograph A picture or drawing used to represent a word or idea.

politics The act of governing a nation.

unify To bring together.

FOR MORE INFORMATION

Amnesty International India
4th Floor, Statesman House
Connaught Place
New Delhi, Delhi
India 110001
Website: http://www.amnesty.org.in
Amnesty International India is a global movement involved in protect-
    ing people who are denied justice or freedom in India.

Anthropological Survey of India (ANSI)
27 Jawaharlal Nehru Road
Kolkata, West Bengal
India 700016
O33-2286 1697
Website: http://www.ansi.gov.in
ANSI pursues anthropological research and projects through the gov-
    ernment of India.

Embassy of India
2107 Massachusetts Avenue NW
Washington, DC 20008
(202) 939-7000
Website: http://www.indianembassy.org
The Indian embassy represents the country of India in the United
    States.

Indian Council for Cultural Relations (ICCR)
Azad Bhavan,
I.P. Estate
New Delhi, Delhi
India 110002
011-23379309, 23379310
Website: http://www.iccr.gov.in
The Indian Council for Cultural Relations forms and implements policies and programs pertaining to India's external cultural relations with other countries

WEBSITES

Because of the changing nature of Internet links, Rosen Publishing has developed an online list of websites related to the subject of this book. This site is updated regularly. Please use this link to access the list:

http://www.rosenlinks.com/SRFAC/idec

FOR FURTHER READING

Dalal, Roshen. *The Puffin History of India for Children, Vol. 1*. Haryana, India: Penguin India, 2003.

Daud, Ali. *Hands-On History! Ancient India: Discover the Rich Heritage of the Indus Valley and the Mughal Empire, with 15 Step-by-Step Projects and 340 Pictures.* Helotes, Texas: Armadillo, 2014.

DK Publishing. *DK Eyewitness Travel Guide: India*. London, England: DK Eyewitness Travel, 2014.

Holm, Kirsten. *Everyday Life in Ancient India* (Jr. Graphic Ancient Civilizations). New York, NY: Powerkids Press, 2012.

Lassier, Allison. *Ancient India* (The Ancient World). New York, NY; Children's Press, 2013.

Lowenstein, Tom. *The Civilization of Ancient India and Southeast Asia* (Illustrated History of the Ancient World). New York, NY: Rosen Publishing Group, 2012.

Mukundan, Monica, and Subhadra Gupta. *Of Kings and Commoners: Fact & Fiction From the Past (2nd Edition).* Delhi, India: Ratna Sagar, 2010.

National Geographic. *Great Empires: An Illustrated Atlas.* Washington, DC: National Geographic Publishing, 2012.

Sharma, Ram Sharan. *Sudras in Ancient India: A Social History of the Lower Order Down to Circa A.D. 600.* New Delhi, India: Motial Banarsidass Publishers, 2014.

Weaver, Stephan. *The History of India in 50 Events: (Indian History–Akbar the Great–East India Company Taj Mahal–Mahatma Gandhi) (*Timeline History in 50 Events Book). Seattle, WA: CreateSpace Independent Publishing Platform, 2015.

BIBLIOGRAPHY

Chaurasia, Radley Shyam. *History of Ancient India*. New Delhi, India: Atlantic Publishers & Distribution, 2002.

Dement, Paul George, and Geoffrey McNicol, editors. *Encyclopedia of Population*. New York, NY: Macmillan Reference USA, 2003.

Hinds, Kathryn. *India's Gupta Dynasty*. Salt Lake City, UT: Benchmark Books, 1996.

Kapur, Kamels. *Portraits of a Nation: History of Ancient India* (Regional National History). New Delhi, India: Sterling Publishers, 2010.

Mookerji, Radhakumud. *Gupta Empire*. New Delhi, India: Motilal Banarsidass Publishers, 2007.

Robinson, Martin. "Scientists Confirm Early Humans Were from Africa but Their Route out Was via Arabia Not Egypt." *Daily Mail*, November 4, 2011. Accessed November 12, 2015 (http://www.dailymail.co.uk/sciencetech/article-2057546/Early-humans-Africa-route-Arabia-Egypt.html).

Rose, Christopher. "Episode 15: The 'Era Between the Empires' of Ancient India." *12 Minute History*. The University of Texas at Austin, March 6, 2013. Accessed November 12, 2015 (http://15minutehistory.org/2013/03/06/episode-15-the-era-between-the-empires-of-ancient-india).

Sacks, David, Oswyn Murray and Lisa R. Brody. *Encyclopedia of the Ancient Greek World*. New York, NY: Facts On File, 2005.

Troutman, Thomas R. *India: Brief History of a Civilization (2nd Edition)*. New York, NY: Oxford University Press, 2015.

Von Pochhammer, William. *India's Road to Nationhood: A Political History of the Subcontinent*. Columbia, MO: South Asia Books, 1993.

Whipps, Heather. "How Ancient Trade Changed the World." *LiveScience*. TechMedia Network, February 17, 2008. Accessed November 15, 2015 (http://www.livescience.com/4823-ancient-trade-changed-world.html)

INDEX

A

Achaemenid Empire, 18, 20
Alexander the Great, 20, 22
Ashoka, 22, 24, 26

B

British East India Company, 38
Buddhism, 24, 28, 32

C

caste system, 16
Chandragupta Maurya, 22
Chandragupta I, 30
Chandragupta II, 30, 34
Cyrus the Great, 18, 20

G

Golden Age, 30, 32, 36
Gupta Empire, 28, 30, 32, 34, 36, 38

H

Hindi, 12
Hinduism, 24, 26, 32

I

Indo-Europeans, 12, 14
Indus Civilization, 8, 10

K

Kalidasa, 32
Kushan, 28

M

Mauryan Empire, 22, 26, 30
Muslim rule, 38, 40

N

Nanda Empire, 20, 22
nomads, 6, 8, 40

P

Persia/Persians, 18, 20, 28

S

Samudrahupta, 30
Sanskrit, 12
Silk Road, 28
Skandagupta, 36

V

Vedas, 14, 24

W

White Huns, 34, 36, 40

ABOUT THE AUTHOR

Kerry Hinton is a writer from Hoboken, NJ. He has always been interested in the development of early man and the first cities and societies on earth. He has visited the Colosseum in Rome as well as the Parthenon in Athens, Greece. On his next trip, to the Indian subcontinent (which will be his first), he plans to visit many of the stops on the Silk Road. His route will take him from the Indus River to the Ganges and east to China.

PHOTO CREDITS